Nadif's New Life

As told to Marilyn Woolley
Photography by Michael Curtain

Contents

Chapter 1: A village in Somalia

My name is Nadif.
I was born in a part of Africa called Somalia.

I lived with my family in a village until I was nine years old.

We lived in a house with a thatched roof. My family grew most of our food in a vegetable garden. We also had lots of farm animals.

My brothers and I looked after the farm animals. When we weren't looking after the farm animals, we played soccer. Soccer was our favourite game.

My life changed forever when I was nine years old. Terrible fighting started. The people who were fighting each other had guns and planes with bombs. Many people were killed and their homes were destroyed.

When the fighting came to my village, I was scared and ran to hide in the forest. I wanted to go back to my village to find my family, but I couldn't because my village had been destroyed.

I was so scared, I ran deeper into the forest. Soon I met up with some other boys who were trying to get away from the fighting, too.

Chapter 2: On the run

The boys told me they were trying to get to a place called Kenya where they would be safe. They said I should go with them. We had to walk deep into the jungle to hide from the people with guns and bombs. We stayed close together and looked after each other.

At night, we slept in the jungle. We were scared because we knew that lions were nearby.

Sometimes, we walked for days without sleeping. We were sad and lonely and missed our families.

When we came to small towns, we stopped and asked for food. We ate bananas and corn but sometimes we only had grass and leaves to eat.

When it rained heavily, we had to walk in deep, fast-flowing water or swim across wide rivers. I was scared of the crocodiles and snakes in the river.

It took us eight weeks to get to Kenya.

Then we went on a bus to a refugee camp. A refugee camp is a place for people who have had to leave their homes.

At the camp, some of the boys found their families, but no one from my family was there.

At the refugee camp, I slept under a plastic shelter.

I did jobs to get money. With the money, I was able to buy food from the markets that people had set up in the camp.

I even went to school in the refugee camp.

Chapter 3: A new family

One day, I was chosen to go and live in Australia. I did not know anything about Australia.

When I arrived in Australia, I lived with a family in a big city.

It was good to be far away from the guns and the bombs in Somalia, but I missed my family.

I had to find out about a lot of new things. I had to study English so I could speak it all the time. I had to find out about the things people did in Australia.

I did this by going to the library to read and borrow books. I also liked finding out how to use a computer.

www.studysearch.com.au

Many things in Australia were different from my old life in my village in Somalia.

The shops and markets were different. I tried hard to remember the names of new types of food, such as mushrooms and broccoli, and I had to get used to different sorts of bread and cakes.

There were so many cars on the wide roads.

I had to find out how to cross the road safely, and how to catch the right bus or train to go places.

Chapter 4: My new life

At my new school, I met lots of new people and I made some new friends.

On the weekends, I liked to go to the park or swim at the swimming pool or at the beach with my friends.

Many games were different from those I played in Somalia. I watched how people played these games and I tried to learn the rules.

But one game was just the same as the one I played in Somalia and at the refugee camp with my old friends.

Soccer is still my favourite game.

A note from the author

I wrote this book because I had worked closely with refugee families after they came to Australia. I was so sad to hear about some of the hardships and troubles they had as they fled their war-torn countries. I was so impressed by their courage and their bravery. I thought it was important to gather stories like this one from Nadif and to tell how young people can advance their lives in new countries if we give them a chance.